The Sky Is Not Always Blue

a collection of poems by

Billie-Jade Locke

with illustrations by Kai Anders

Contents

CHAPTER 3

Introduction

Throughout my life I've found it hard to express my emotions. I don't have a big group of friends; I don't like being the centre of attention, and I still face anxiety over small things every single day. I was afraid of telling people how I was feeling and what I had been through in the past in case I wouldn't fit in or they would judge me.

I went through a rough patch and poetry was my way of expressing the anger and pain inside me. Writing has been my cathartic release. Although my poems are not filled with images of sunshine and words of happiness, they are raw emotion and every poem carries a message.

Living with a mental illness is never easy, and the stigma surrounding mental illness needs to come to an end. I hope that somewhere in this collection you can relate, find some understanding of mental illness or gain some inspiration yourself. Never be ashamed of who you are.

Billie-Jade Locke
Guernsey, May 2020

CHAPTER 1

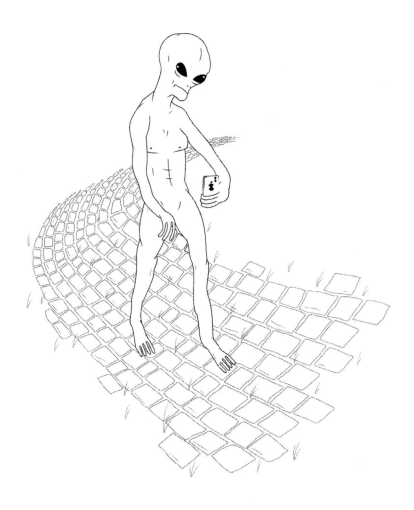

We are our own enemy

How do you erase the grey without a rubber?
There's lots of evil in this world, so much betrayal.
Children should have freedom to play.
Not have to worry, "Will I be shot at school today?"

We walk these streets, not making eye contact.
It's alien if you smile.
What did money and stigma do to us?
People only care about their social profile.

Technology is advancing quicker than we blink.
People pay the price, say it's great..but let's think.
The more machines we have, the less jobs available.
It will become a trial of the human most assailable.

This world is becoming ugly, soon it will end.
It's our fault for overusing resources just to fit in with the new trend.

Social Stigma

We live in a world, everything judged by society.
The way we look, how we feel, what we eat and our propriety.

There is a stigma in mental illness, making people afraid
of their mind.
Afraid to speak up about how they are feeling, fearing
they'll be defined.

When people are diagnosed, they believe this is their
personality.
When someone breaks a limb, we don't put them
in a category.
So why do we do this with people's mentality?

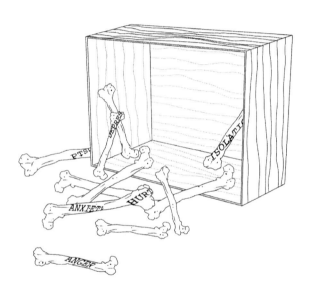

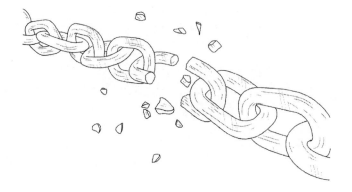

Lost Independence

Loneliness is one of the worst feelings we endure,
unlike physical pain it's not something we can cure.

Born into this world, with plenty of places to roam.
Always searching for something to comfort us,
so we will never feel alone.

When did humans become so dependent on each other?
Our independence fading away, now all we do is smother.

Someone else's addiction

You don't have friends, no one can relate.
You became a carer for your mother at the age of
just eight.

When you live with a parent whose addiction is a
substance, that's poisoning their insides and mind.
You look at the world differently.
You lose yourself, becoming a human who feels your
purpose has already been assigned.

Some parts of you are afraid one day the addiction
will kill them.
The rest of you wishes it would all just end for good.
You were only eight years old when you became an
adult, losing the rest of your childhood.

The Taste

I listen to loud music, to drown out the sound.
The devil keeps shouting, my head starts to pound.
I wonder when good thoughts will start happening,
all these bad ones make me remember the kidnapping.
I've been robbed of my social life, childhood as well.
My mother's an alkie… I'm living in hell.

She'll always love the taste more than me,
she's been to self-help groups can no one see,
that she's dying inside and feeling crappy?
She's lying to you all to keep you happy.

She's tried suicide countless times.
Why does she let alcohol poison her mind?
She's not the only one living with the devil, she's selfish
and careless on a whole new level.
You've turned your child's life upside down.
Please pick yourself up, don't choose to drown.

At a party

When I drink alcohol, I feel like my mother.
I think people look at me, ask themselves,
"Who will ever love her?"

I prefer to stand alone, closely holding my drink.
Tears start in my eyes, I quickly try to blink.
They ask, 'Are you happy, will you dance?'
but I stand still, like I'm in a trance.
I want to have fun, let myself free.
but I'm afraid I will find my mother in me.

CHAPTER 2

-1 degree

I am not cold because outside it is -1 degree,
I am cold because overnight anxiety consumed me.
It shivers down my spine, and then I freeze.
I want to be happy and healthy, to smile with ease.
I always have my headphones in my ears,
I hope no one judges my music if they hear.
I'm always conscious of what I wear,
I think they are judging me, but why would they care?
I find it hard to have motivation, when all I want is to
sink to the bottom of the ocean.

Trapped

She's trying to find methods, coping strategies ...
She can't stop thinking about all her abnormalities.

She hates herself more with every breath she takes.
She hates herself more for not ending it ... for your sake.

She doesn't know why she bothers with daily activities,
when all she wishes is to embrace her negativity.

Some days it's harder, some days It's even worse,
Some days she feels like she's trapped in a curse.

Wonder

I wonder if one day, I'll wake up and the world will feel different?
If the sky will stay blue and depression becomes non-existent.
I wonder if I'll be able to hold a smile without this aching inside?
Tell people I'm okay and not feel like I've lied.
I wonder if I'll wake up actually wanting to be here?
Have real friends, who are not insincere.
Is this day coming near? Because I am getting worse and I'm living in fear.

Tsunami

The sadness inside is like a tsunami, a wave taking over
her body and mind.
Being around people or sitting alone, it doesn't make a
difference, nowhere feels like home.

She's lived with depression for a long time,
thinking it's a normal feeling to want to die,
she sits in her room losing track of time.

Staring into nothing for hours and hours,
not thinking or feeling as her own mind devours.
I guess the thoughts that are destroying her mind,
will always be the words unspoken and unkind.

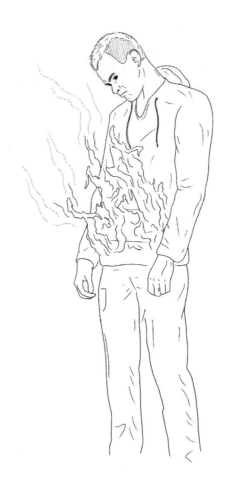

The Urge

The urge to self-harm never fully goes away.
Scars covering her body remind her every day.
She has strategies and methods to help her unwind,
but she can still feel the desire deep inside her mind.

People who never felt the relief as she has, will never
quite understand.
How she can harm herself, blood running down her hands.
Never get mad at people for not understanding why,
not everyone will understand the feeling of needing to satisfy.

No way out

The feeling just won't go away,
it depresses her every single day.
She thinks about self-harm and suicide often,
she's thought about the way she'll look in her coffin.
Self-harm and suicide flood in her head,
all those words spoken but none of them said.
Her life keeps turning into a disaster, time needs to stop
but it keeps getting faster.
They don't call it committing suicide anymore, they call
it completion. That's what you are remembered for.

All those famous people not remembered for their art,
but only remembered for ways they chose to depart.

Justify me

She feels dead inside but getting rid of her corpse could
never be justified.
It's difficult when in life you have more than most,
but all she wishes is to be nothing more than
a forgotten ghost.

People often say she's ungrateful for feeling that way,
she is not ungrateful... She's struggling.
I hope you notice that one day.
She forces herself to do things that she never wanted to do.
In hope that one day those skies will turn blue.

Embedded

If I had a choice in life, it would be to get rid of the
demons embedded in my mind.
They are not welcome here, but have found a place to hide.

They thrive on the darkness.
I feel it moving throughout my body, just beneath the skin.
It burns from deep inside; I feel the need to release the
demons buried within.

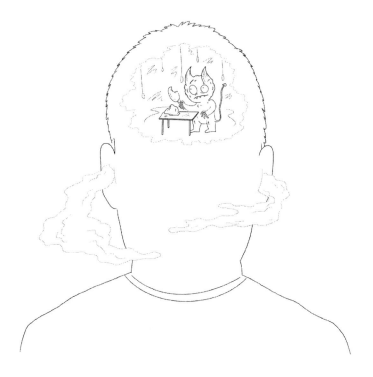

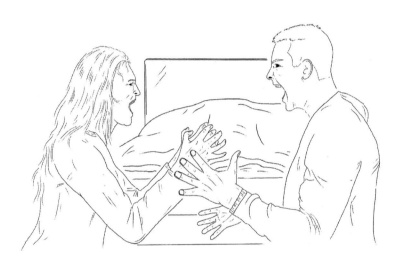

I'd rather be

You're always asking her, "When's the next time you're getting out of bed?"
She gets angry and shouts back at you. "I'D RATHER BE DEAD!"

The pillow and duvet are the only company she desires.
The warmth and beating of another human is not what she requires.

You don't get it. She wants to lay there. Pretend that she's not breathing.
She hopes you never have to experience that deep, dark, empty feeling.

Fix me

No one can fix you, are they aware?
Look behind the broken smiles, don't bully for a dare.
Taking a blade to their wrist, the blood running down
their arms.
This is the story as to why they self-harm.
Voices in their head, demons in their blood.
When will it end, they've had enough.
"Everything is okay, everything is fine
sit back and relax, smile... don't cry."

They get called fakers but can no one see?
This isn't the way they wanted to be.
They can't stop crying, thinking they're insane.
They want out of this life so they feel no more pain.

"Everything is now better.
I'm sorry for being vain
but at least you won't have to see me.
Maybe you're aware I am nothing but memories now
of people who I thought didn't care."

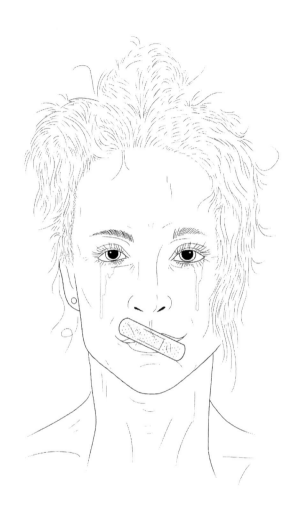

Poker face

Her skin is so pale, scars cover her arms.
She mumbles words, doesn't want to self harm.
She hates attention, she cowers away.
She doesn't speak up, when she's not okay.
She avoids interaction, it gives her chills.
How do people actually enjoy this thrill?

She's never relaxed, it's always on her mind.
She's always fidgeting with anything she can find.
The older she becomes, the worse it gets.
She feels as though her life is falling to bits.
She's got a good poker face,in the hope you won't know.
That all of her demons are hidden below.

Black sweater

It's hard living in a world where everything seems so
dull and grey.
I try to concentrate on the happier things but my mind
gets led astray.
I always wear black sweaters so you don't see the tears
on my sleeve.
When I say I'm fine, you know it's not true and still you
choose to leave.
I hear a lot of people saying they think it's just a phase.
Why tell them any different when 'It's just one of those days?'

Feelings of nothing

When I felt sadness, I felt happiness sometimes too.
Then I took those tablets, I felt numb the whole way through.
I was just organs, working with a blank mind.
I couldn't sleep or eat. I was zombified.

I was addicted to the darkness that followed me around.
Even my favourite songs had no meaning, it was just sound.
My head hurt from frowning, trying to recover my thoughts.
They used to flow like a river, but now are frozen like a lake.
Maybe one day the cycle of feeling nothing will break.

Alone is to be free

I have blocked out my feelings for far too long,
that now I start to feel anything but numb
I feel in this world, I don't belong.

For me it is easier to be alone, for no one to care.
When people get close, they think they know me
they don't, I'm suffocating, I need air.

I take breaths from deep within to refill the air escaping me.
Finally, I should learn that being alone is the best way to be.

Reflection

There is a ghost in the mirror, is that ghost me?
I don't know who I am or who I'm supposed to be.
When I smile, I know it's fake.
Real smiles are the ones that ache.
I don't know who I am or who I'm supposed to be.
I guess that ghost in the mirror really is me.

Forever alone

The realisation of having no one is finally hitting me.
I shut myself out completely, spending my time
watching the sea.
The waves crashing around me are the only thing to
keep me company.

Talking with waves is not the same as talking with people.
Waves stay when it's rough,
people run away.
Which is why the friends I make, would never know the
real me.
In hope they might stay.

Fading

The depression that consumed me was part of my identity for so many years.
That losing the part of myself that I knew so well was one of my biggest fears.

Blue skies are becoming visible, my depression is fading away.
I'm scared to see the happy me, and what that will portray.

Am I changing?

Today I achieved something that I haven't before,
it was the one day I remember not feeling numb to the core.
I laughed with people, we joked a lot,
I had no feelings of my body wanting to rot.
Maybe this is the day, where things start to change.
That my mind can rest and stop acting so strange.
This is the first evening I haven't wanted to die,
in such a long time... I didn't even cry.
I hope this feeling stays inside me,
it feels like my mind could finally be set free.

Mind like a tide

Depression is like an ocean, tides crashing back and
forth in your mind.
You don't have control over it, your feelings and body
are both confined.
You can almost see it disappearing, then suddenly it's
crashing back.
It's like your mind and the ocean have a constant plan
of attack.
The tide always comes in quickly but then it lingers.
You get feelings you thought were gone.
You see old memories, all those bad triggers.
Don't go in the ocean, unless you can swim away from
the dark patch.
Because once you touch the dark, it will suddenly latch.
The ocean is a rough place, and escaping is never as
easy as you think.
Fighting tides are tiring, but don't let yourself sink.

Faced with fear

I am not afraid of becoming sad again, but it seems to terrify you.
I think you are afraid to wake up one day, with my funeral to attend to.

You are afraid because my sadness is nothing like yours.
Your sadness is water in a river passing by,
my sadness is an ocean in which I'm drowning with every sigh.

Panic

I will never get used to the feeling of having a panic attack.
All bad memories each time, keep coming back.

One day you feel like you can conquer the world,
the next day you're a crying mess in the corner curled.

We need to appreciate the small things we tend to forget.
Not hate ourselves for the small things we feel we regret.

Clouds are funny

Although some days the skies are still grey,
my mind has finally stopped torturing me.
Most negative thoughts are easy to fade away.

The clouds resemble my thoughts, in funny shapes both
big and small.
The days that I feel best are when there are no clouds at all.

Leave me free

The depression that had once consumed my body,
has now left me be.
It's left me feeling happy,
Left me feeling free.

CHAPTER 3

Be with me

When I look into your eyes I get so lost in time,
nothing else matters, everything with you is perfect and
sublime.
We learn about each other, so we know how to love
one another.
When you start learning together you uncover secrets
and start to discover.
You learn new things about yourself, that you never
knew before.
I want to spend my entire life with you, nothing less ...
only more.

Broken promises

You promised me that you would never let anything
hurt me, including you.
Oh, the pain you gave me... proved all those words you
said to be untrue.
I think the pain makes me stronger, but at the same
time I feel weak.
How did you ruin something which was so beautifully unique?
How can you knowingly hurt someone so much and say
you still care, if this is what we call love?
Our love is not fair.

LOVE

2 AM

She still remembers the night you told her, you were
stuck in traffic at 2 in the morning.
She should've realised that night what had happened,
but she ignored every warning.
You said you missed her, as your fingers were touching
another person's skin.
Whilst you kissed and gave pleasure to another body,
you told her how you loved her deep within.

You came home and told how wonderful she is,
that she should never let your love go.
You said you'd never hurt her, that same night you
travelled to meet her again.
Like your love was just a game show.
The thought of you touching another woman's body,
the way you did hers
will forever make her sick inside.
Cheating should be a crime, for it can never be justified.

Attacked by own trust

Trust is not something that comes easily.
It takes time to get to know someone, and trust each
other evenly.
When you start to trust that person, you put your
feelings on the line.
When one person lies to you, breaks your bond.
Subconsciously you will untwine.

The trust you once had before, you will never have back.
You keep your walls built strong, in case of another attack.
It is sad when someone's walls have been cracked so
much it hurts them to trust.
No one should be hurt in this way, with their heart
being crushed.

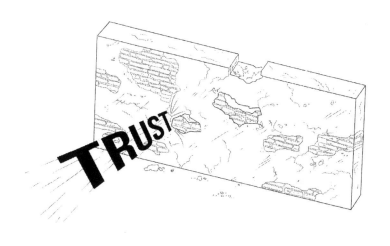

TRUST

Blinded by you

The day you told me, all I wanted was for you to explain.
How the love of my life betrayed me,
lost our love and caused me immense pain.

The moment those words came out of your mouth,
I wanted to become deaf.
I was already blinded by you, the ache in my heart
was all I had left.

I tried to put the pieces together, understand it in a way
I could process.
But in my mind the image of you and her together is
something I can never suppress

Doubts in her mind

"All I wanted was love," she says as she's choking on her
tears at 2am in the morning.
The memories of you hurting her, take over without warning.
"It's probably my own fault," she blames herself for the
actions you used to disrespect her.
She starts to hate herself, she can't remember the last
happy moment, it's a blur.

"Was she better than me?" she asks this question a
thousand times, making herself crazy.
The only thing she can think about is you touching
another woman's body.
"Did he even love me?" she doubts every word he ever said.
"Am I capable of being loved by someone who won't
hurt me again?"
All these questions on a constant cycle in her head.

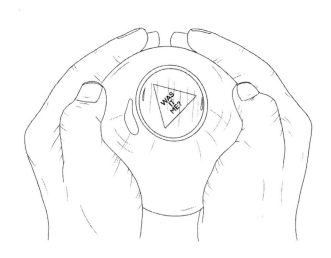

He Will

He will tell you all the things you want to hear.
He will make you feel things you never have before my dear.
He will make you blind, make you never doubt a word he said.
He will manipulate you, all those red flags you never read.
He will one day wonder if he has all he can possibly need.
He will realise he wants more, knowing he's hurting you, but
still proceeds.
He will try to hide the fact he has done anything wrong.
He will notice you're blind, he still plays along.
He is the worst type of person, yet you don't realise,
this isn't what love is supposed to be.
But when you finally realise, my dear you'll be free.

Love me

Long distance relationships aren't made to be easy,
but the feelings I get from you are the best I've felt
inside of me.
I wished to find someone to love me, and not punish me
for my past.
To learn everything about each other, see a perfect contrast.

When my tears were falling on your chest,
it was at that moment I knew my feelings were starting
to manifest.
When I told you I loved you, it all became clear.
That I didn't need to wish any longer, I had what I
always wanted here.

81

The One

The one

You told me you loved me, that I am 'the one' for you.
I feel the same way, but I warn you ... my skies are not blue.

I have cloudy days painted with different shades of grey,
but maybe you're my Van Gogh and the blue will stay.